W9-BAQ-103

Presented to

From

Date

A Celebration of Motherhood

Haden
Harris Pickel
& Annette
Crivella Williams

Fleming H. Revell
A Division of Baker Book House Co
Grand Rapids, Michigan 49516

© 1994 Haden Harris Pickel and Annette Crivella Williams

ISBN 0-8007-7212-1

Published by Fleming H. Revell
a division of Baker Book House Company
P.O. Box 6287, Grand Rapids, Michigan 49516-6287

PRINTED IN THE UNITED STATES OF AMERICA
Every effort was made to locate Copyright holders of materials used in this book. We apologize for any errors or omissions and will be happy to make corrections in future printing or editions.

Book Development by March Media, Inc.
Book Design by Brenda Pope Design
Production by Bozeman Design

All rights reserved. No part of this publication may be reproduced, storied in a retrieval system, or transmitted in any form or by any means—electronic, mechanical, photocopy, recording, or any other—without the prior permission of the publisher. The only exception is brief quotations in printed reviews.

Scripture quotations are taken from the King James Version of the Bible.

This book is dedicated to our dear mothers,

Ellen Louise Furman Crivella
and
Lillian Boyd Haden Harris

*whose gentle love and guidance
inspired this book.*

CONTENTS

*I*n all the world there is no relationship more precious than that of the mother and child. Thoughts of mother and home awaken the deepest emotions that stir within us. At no time in history has this relationship been more sacred than during the Victorian era. In researching this book we were deeply moved by the beautiful poetry and prose written during that period in tribute to motherhood.

It was believed that next to the sovereign grace of God, a mother's example was most effective in molding character and shaping destiny; and no influence in the universe contributed so much toward guiding immortal souls heavenward as that of the mother.

Whether we are birth mothers, adoptive mothers, godmothers, aunts, friends, or cousins, there is deep within us a nurturing spirit that can make a difference in the life of a child, thus enriching our own lives.

This book is set forth in the hope that it may awaken the reader to a deeper appreciation of mothers; that it may strengthen family bonds, making them more beautiful and tender; and that it will return us to a more compassionate society. For as the mother is the fountainhead of the household, it is equally true that the household is the fountainhead of society.

At the close of the book we have provided blank pages entitled "Memories of My Mother." We hope you will record memories of your own mother in this space, thus making this book your personal celebration of motherhood.

Haden and Ann

FROM A
MOTHER'S HEART
AS SHE
AWAITS HER BABY

*As I wait for your arrival—
sometimes patiently, sometimes not so
patiently—I wonder what you will be
like. I feel you move inside me and your
heart beat next to mine. I know you are
part of me; yet I also remind myself that
you are your own little person, a divine
inspiration of God. I can't wait to meet
you; I already love you.*

$\mathcal{B}$ut one thing on earth is better than the wife;
that is the mother.

Leopold Schaefer

$\mathcal{H}$e shall feed his flock like a shepherd:
he shall gather the lambs with his arm,
and carry them in his bosom, and shall
gently lead those that are with young.

Isaiah 40:11

$\mathcal{I}$ am the mother of an immortal being!
God be merciful to me a sinner!

Margaret Fuller Ossoli

THE LITTLE PEOPLE

A dreary place would this earth be
Were there no little people in it;
The song of life would lose its mirth,
Were there no children to begin it.

No little forms, like buds to grow,
And make the admiring heart surrender;
No little hands on breast and brow,
To keep the thrilling love-chords tender.

The sterner souls would grow more stern.
Unfeeling nature more inhuman,
And man to stoic coldness turn,
And woman would be less than woman.

Life's song, indeed, would lose its charm,
Were there no babies to begin it;
A doleful place this world would be,
Were there no little people in it.

John Greenleaf Whittier

THE
ANTICIPATION
OF BIRTH

*U*nlike today when a woman knows almost immediately, a woman of earlier times could not be certain of pregnancy until around the third month. Based on her suspicions, she would seek a doctor's confirmation.

Doctors of the era generally gave advice about diet, exercise, rest, diversion, fresh air, and sunshine. A daily dose of cod liver oil was also often prescribed. Once her "delicate" condition was diagnosed, she was encouraged by both physician and acquaintances to conserve her strength by resting several times during the day.

$\mathcal{T}$he mother's love is at first an absorbing delight, blunting all other sensibilities; it is an expansion of the animal existence; it enlarges the imagined range for self to move in; but in after years it can only continue to be joy on the same terms as other long-lived love; that is, by much suppression of self, and power of living in the experience of another.

George Eliot

$\mathcal{A}$nd whoso shall receive one such little child in my name receiveth me.

Matthew 18:5

When among all life's miracles I try
What highest argument may certify
That God is good, however things may seem,
On this I rest, and evil dims like dream —
Each little soul that voyages toward birth,
When it arrives on earth,
Makes gentlest landfall on a mother's breast.

William C. Gannett

And Adam called his wife's name Eve;
because she was the mother of all living.

Genesis 3:20

Eve was made of a rib out of the
side of Adam, not made out of
his head to top him, nor out of
his feet to be trampled upon by
him, but out of his side to be
equal with him, under his arm to
be protected, and near his heart
to be beloved.

Matthew Henry

A WOMAN'S HEART

God's angels took a little drop of dew
Fresh fallen from the heaven's far-off blue,
And a white violet, so pure and bright,
Shedding its fragrance in the morn's soft light,
And a forget-me-not laid altogether gently out of
    sight
Within the chalice of a lily white.
With humbleness and grace they covered it,
Made purity and sadness near to sit,
And added pride to this and fears a few,
One wish, but half a hope, and bright tears, too,
Courage and sweetness in misfortune's smart,
And out of this they molded woman's heart.

Lo, children are a heritage of the Lord;
and the fruit of the womb is his reward.

Psalm 127:3

MOTHER LOVE

I gave my maiden love tender and shy,
And yet I was sad. Why? O why?

I gave my wife love pure and true,
And yet — and yet I was longing too!

God gave me mother-love warm and strong,
And my sadness was lost in my lullaby song.

F. T. Morgan

Is not a young mother one of the sweetest
sights which life shows us?

William Makepeace Thackeray

IN A
FAMILY WAY

In Victorian times sharing the news of a coming baby was momentous. In a time when intimate matters were not discussed, terms like "in a family way" were used to describe a woman's sensitive condition.

Most women had their babies at home under the watchful eye of a midwife, neighbor, or friend. It was a rare community that had a resident doctor.

The time of birth was always of great concern because of the high rate of infant mortality and danger to the mother as well.

For many expectant mothers, confinement to home and bed was prescribed. Her hours were occupied with preparation for the birthing process and fashioning baby's layette. Thus she readied herself mentally and physically as she anticipated the days ahead.

And a little child shall lead them.

Isaiah 11:6

There is perhaps no such moment of
exquisite joy, of deep unutterable
thanksgiving taking the place of pain and
sorrow, as when a woman knows herself
to be the living mother of a living child.

Andrew Murray

A mother's first ministration for her infant is to
enter, as it were, the valley of the shadow of
death, and win its life at the peril of her own.
How different must an affection thus founded be
from all others!

Mrs. Sigourney

BREATHE A PRAYER

*Y*ou who lie beneath my heart,
In whose soul I have no part;
Whose sweet shape will someday rest
Close, ah close! against my breast —
Breathe a prayer to God for me
That I love you worthily.

You whose eyes I have not seen,
Yet whose sight will be so keen
When you come to judge my life
With its foolishness and strife —
Breathe a prayer to God for me
That he give you Charity.

Anonymous

AS SHE AWAITS HER BABY

NAMING
THE BABY

There was much deliberation about the choice of a baby's name. In that era it was important that a boy's name be strong and a girl's name be feminine. Coupled with this was the emphasis on family tradition that often meant passing a name from one generation to the next.

Unlike today when the baby's gender is known prior to birth, the Victorians were surprised with the sex of their child. Therefore, it was necessary to have chosen both a boy's name and a girl's name. Many families did not speak the baby's name until the christening service, so the child was simply called Baby.

Popular Names
of the Victorian Era
and Their
Meanings

Parents were aware that a name stayed with the child throughout life. Great care was given to selecting a name with a meaning which exemplified the traits that a parent wished the child to have. Below is a list of some of the more popular names of the time.

Abigail — a father's joy
Drusilla — strong
Ellen — bright one
Enid — spotless purity
Frederica — peaceful ruler
Grace — thanks
Hannah —grace
Inez — sacred
Julia — soft haired or youthful one
Victoria —conqueror

Albert — noble
Charles — strong, manly
Clarence — famous one
Edward — guardian
Ernest — earnest one
James — the supplanter
Joseph — he shall add
Leon — lion
Nathaniel — a gift from God
William — protector

From a Mother's Heart after the Baby Arrives

As I gaze into your eyes and count your tiny fingers and toes, I can't believe your perfection. You are actually here. I am overwhelmed at how helpless you are and at my responsibility to anticipate your every need. When you cry, my heart skips a beat. When you don't cry, I worry too. I don't know how to be a mother yet. Lord, can I?

SINCE BABY CAME

Since Baby came
The birds all sing a brighter, merrier lay.
The weary, darksome shades have fled away,
And night has blossomed into perfect day
Since Baby came.

Florence Catherine Baird

Wherefore it came to pass, when the time was
come about after Hannah had conceived, that
she bare a son, and called his name Samuel,
saying, "Because I have asked him of the
Lord."

1 Samuel 1:20

A CURLY LAMB

Angels at the foot,
And angels at the head,
And like a curly little lamb
My pretty babe in bed.

Christina Rossetti

THE NEWBORN BABE

*I*nto our home one blessed day
A wee sweet babe had found its way.
While through the mist of tears and
   pain,
Sunlight fell on our hearts again.

Mother! To thee this day is given
A soul to keep and fit for heaven.
Oh, watch and lead the little feet
Through the day's toil, and pain, and
   heat,
Lest from the path they go astray
And wander from God's fold away.
And guide the hands that they may
   know
No other will than His below.
And train the heart so pure and mild
Into the likeness of the Child
Who came into this world of sin
And gave His life our souls to win.
Heed well the charge! Nor hope to
   plead,
Thou couldst not know, thou didst
   not heed.

Marion Longfellow

A BABY
HAS COME!

Men and women of the previous century were reluctant to discuss matters pertaining to sexual relations with their children. However, when a baby arrived, an explanation was needed for other children in the household or neighborhood.

The Victorians conveniently adoped the old Dutch myth that babies were brought by the stork. This large white bird had many of the qualities much admired by the moralistic Victorians.

The stork was monogamous, cared for its young, and returned to nest in the same chimney year after year.

The American Victorians furthered the stork tradition by embellishing baby books, announcements, and congratulatory cards with this gawky symbolic bird.

BABY'S SKIES

Would you know the baby's skies?
Baby's skies are mother's eyes.
Mother's eyes and smile together
Make the baby's pleasant weather.

Mother, keep your eyes from tears.
Keep your heart from foolish fears.
Keep your lips from dull complaining,
Lest the baby think 'tis raining.

Mary C. Bartlett

ONLY A BABY SMALL

Only a baby small,
  Dropt from the skies;
Only a laughing face,
  Two sunny eyes.
Only two cherry lips,
  One chubby nose;
Only two little hands,
  Ten little toes.
Only a golden head,
  Curly and soft;
Only a tongue that wags,
  Loudly and oft.
Only a little brain,
  Empty of thought;
Only a little heart,
  Troubled with naught.
Only a baby small,
  Never at rest;
Small but how dear to us,
  God knoweth best.
Only a tender flower
  Sent us to rear;
Only a life to love
  While we are here.

Mathias Barr

All hopes and loves unworthy
Fade out at this sweet hour;
All pure and noble longings
Renew their holy power;
For Christ, who in the Virgin
Our motherhood has blest,
Is near to every woman
With a baby on her breast.

Mary Frances Butts

A babe is mother's anchor.

Henry Ward Beecher

A mother's arms are made of tenderness
and children sleep soundly in them.

Victor Hugo

TO VEGA

*A*ll heaven and immortality
In my baby's eyes do lie,
Pools of starlit mystery.

Tell me, baby, you who've known
Dim blue distances star-strown,
Are unborn babies sad and lone?

Or do they laugh in gleeful mirth?
Are they eager for their birth,
Glad to see the sweet, green earth?

Ah! you listen, stretch your fingers.
Is it toward unearthly singers
Round whose songs your memory lingers?

Yon candle fluttering in the wind
You watch, as though there crossed your mind
A vision of star-flames left behind.

Bright soul, new stranded on life's beach,
What wealth of wisdom you might teach
Could we unlock the gates of speech!

Your crooning of that never-land,
Alas! we cannot understand.
We can but kiss your tiny hand.

Muriel Nelson d'Auvergue

$\mathcal{T}$hou hast covered me in my mother's womb. I will praise thee; for I am fearfully and wonderfully made: marvelous are thy works; and that my soul knoweth right well. My substance was not hid from thee when I was made in secret... How precious also are thy thoughts unto me, O God! How great is the sum of them.

Psalm 139:13-17

There is a sight all hearts beguiling —
A youthful mother to her infant smiling,
Who, with spread arms and dancing feet,
And cooing voice, returns its answer sweet.

Joanna Baillie

A Babe in a house is a wellspring of pleasure,
A messenger of peace and love,
A resting place for innocence on earth;
A link between angels and men.

M. F. Tupper

In Ireland they have a pretty fancy
that when a babe smiles in its sleep
it's talking with angels.

An Irish Proverb

BARTHOLOMEW

Bartholomew is very sweet,
From sandy hair to rosy feet.

Bartholomew is six months old,
And dearer far than pearls or gold.

Bartholomew has deep blue eyes,
Round pieces dropped from out the skies.

Bartholomew is hugged and kissed!
He loves a flower in either fist.

Bartholomew's my saucy son;
No mother has a sweeter one!

Norman Gale

THE LAYETTE

When the baby arrived, much time and labor had already been invested in preparing the nursery and layette. There were many essential garments needed for the new little one, most of which had been lovingly fashioned by Mother's own hands.

A small sampling of items in the layette included:

4 dozen diapers
3 pair of long hose
3 nightgowns
3 cotton wrapping blankets
3 towels
6 washcloths
2 bath blankets
1 baby bunting or snuggle rug
1 bar of baby soap
1 can of baby talcum powder
1 package of boric acid
1 hot water bottle
Olive oil or cocoa butter

In an age when washing machines were a rarity and trips to the store were made on a weekly basis at the most, the above list was just about enough!

A young mother, with her baby in her arms, is ever a means of drawing human thoughts toward that Mother and that Babe who stand forever as our conception of the meeting-point of earth and heaven.

"C."

*A*nd so it was, that, while they were there, the days were accomplished that she should be delivered. And she brought forth her first-born son, and wrapped him in swaddling clothes, and laid him in a manger.

Luke 2: 6-7

*T*he bairn that is born on the Sabbath
    day,
Is lucky and bonny and blithe and gay.
Monday's bairn is fair of face;
Tuesday's bairn is full of grace;
Wednesday's bairn need fear no foe;
Thursday's bairn has far to go;
Friday's bairn is loving and giving.
But Saturday's bairn must work for his
    living.

Anonymous

From a Mother's Heart at the Miracle of a Child

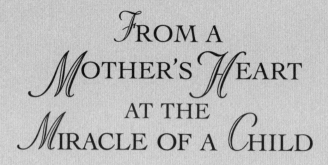

Do you have your father's nose? Do you look like me? What will you look like when you grow up? Your looks change daily; every day brings new delights.

What a wondrous thing a baby is: the sweet smell of your baby head, the hundred little creases in your neck, the dimple in your chin, your eyelashes on your cheek as you sleep . . .

I am in awe.

WEIGHING THE BABY

How many pounds does Baby weigh,
Baby who came awhile ago,
How many pounds from crowning curl
To rosy point of restless toe?
Nobody weighed the Baby's smile,
Or the love that came with the helpless one;
Nobody weighed the thread of care
From which a human life is spun.
Nobody weighed the Baby's soul,
For here on earth no weights there be —
That could avail: God only knows
Its value through eternity.

Anonymous

His mother kept all these sayings in her heart.

Luke 2:51

A NECKLACE

*N*o rubies of red for my lady,
No jewel that glitters and charms—
But the light of the skies,
In a little one's eyes,
And a necklace of two little arms.

Of two little arms that are clinging,
(Oh ne'er was a necklace like this!)
And the wealth of the world,
And love's sweetness impearled,
In the joy of a little one's kiss.

A necklace of love for my lady,
That was linked by the angels above—
No other but this,
And a tender, sweet kiss,
That sealeth a little one's love.

Frank L. Stanton

LEARNING TO WALK

Only beginning the journey,
Many a mile to go,
Little feet, how they patter,
Wandering to and fro.

Trying again so bravely,
Laughing in baby glee;
Hiding its face in Mother's lap,
Proud as a baby can be.

Tottering now and falling,
Eyes that are going to cry,
Kisses and plenty of love words,
Willing again to try.

Father of all, oh, guide them,
The pattering little feet,
While they are treading the uphill road,
Braving the dust and heat.

Aid them when they grow weary,
Keep them in pathway blest,
And when the journey's ended,
Saviour, oh, give them rest.

George Cooper

TWO LITTLE FEET

Two little feet so small
That both may nestle
In one caressing hand,
Two tender feet upon
The untried border
Of life's mysterious land.

Dimpled and soft and pink
As peach tree blossoms
In April's fragrant days,
How can they walk among the briery tangles
Edging the world's tough ways?

Anonymous

COUNTING BABY'S TOES

Dear little bare feet
Dimpled and white,
In your long nightgown
Wrapped for the night.
Come, let me count all
Your queer little toes
Pink as the heart
Of a shell or a rose.

One is a lady
That sits in the sun;
Two is a baby,
And three is a nun;
Four is a lily
With innocent breast.
And five is a birdie
Asleep on her nest.

Anonymous

THE TODDLER'S REIGN

*I*ndoors and out, early and late,
There is no limit to his sway,
For wrapt in baby robes of state
He governs night and day;
Kisses he takes as rightful due,
And Turklike has his slaves to dress him;
His subjects bend before him too.
I'm one of them. God bless him!

John Davis

O chaser of the dragonflies at play,
O son, my son!
I wonder where thy little feet today
Have run!

From the Japanese

MOTHER'S KISSES

They're good for bumps and good for lumps,
They're even good for dumps and grumps,
They're good for stings of bumblebees
And barks from shinnying cherry trees.
For splinters, sunburn, "skeeter-bites,"
For injured feelings after fights,
And scratches, scratched while Tabby hisses —
Mother's kisses.

There's naught so pure, there's naught so sure,
Indeed, they seem a heavenly cure,
For pounded fingers, and stubbed toes,
And all the long, long list of woes.
Yet did you ever think it queer
That while they're fine for every fear
They're just as fine with all the blisses —
Mother's kisses.

Annie Balcomb Wheeler

BATHING
THE BABY

Mothers in Victorian times placed a great emphasis on the cleanliness of their homes and those who lived there. Baby was bathed every day, even though tub baths were not an everyday occurrence.

The infant's bath was almost a ceremonial ritual. Baby's room was second in cleanliness only to an operating room. All Baby's items for the bath were readied, and Baby's clothing was arranged in the order in which it was to be put on: shirt, diaper, long stockings, pettishirt, then dress. The baby's blanket, bath towel, face towel, and washcloth were warmed and laid out.

A large galvanized tub was brought in from outside and filled with heated water. The tub was filled three-quarters full of water, warm when tested with the elbow (about 105° Fahrenheit).

Once this had been completed, baby was prepared for the bath. While Baby was still bundled, Mother cleansed and moistened with oil the child's eyes, ears, and face. Then she washed and patted dry the scalp.

Before Baby was placed in the tub, special attention was given to the little creases of the neck, under the arms, the creases of the elbow, the palms of the hand, and the tiny regions between the fingers and toes. Baby was then placed in the tub, with careful support for the head and shoulders.

Baby was left in the tub only two to three minutes, then removed, wrapped in the warm bath towels and gently patted dry. A tiny bit of oil was carefully rubbed over the child's body to keep his skin soft. Baby was then dressed and ready for the day.

THE FIRST TOOTH

Come, look at the dainty darling,
As fresh as a new-blown rose.
From the top of his head so golden,
To the dear little restless toes.
You can tell by the dancing dimples,
By the smiles that come and go,
He is keeping a wonderful secrct
You'd give half your kingdom to know.

Now kiss him on cheek and forehead
And kiss him on lip and chin.
The little red mouth is hiding
The rarest of pearls within.
Ah, see! When the lips in smiling
Have parted their tender red,
Do you see the tiny white jewel
Set deep in its coral bed?

Now, where are the sage reporters,
Who wait by hamlet and hill
To tell to the listening nations
The news of its good or ill?
Come, weave with your idle gossip
This golden blossom of truth:
Just half a year old this morning
And one little pearly tooth!

Anonymous

MY THUMB, MY TREASURE

If a babe suck his thumb
'Tis an ease to his gum;
A comfort, a boon,
A calmer of grief,
A friend in his need affording relief;
A solace, a good, a soother of pain,
A composer to sleep
A charm and a gain.

Anonymous

LITTLE THINGS

When God makes a lovely thing,
The fairest and completest,
He makes it little, don't you know,
For little things are sweetest.

Little birds and little flowers,
Little diamonds, little pearls:
But the dearest things on earth
Are the little boys and girls.

Anonymous

*M*others in Victorian times began their day very early and without the benefit of modern conveniences. In many cases water had to be pumped from outside the house and brought in for cooking, bathing, and cleaning. Clothes were usually boiled outside in large black kettles or in washtubs over open fires and hung to dry on clotheslines. The family, usually large, had to be fed without benefit of prepared or frozen foods.

The many tasks to be performed to maintain a home and the strict division of labor between the genders meant that a mother might have special preferences for a boy or girl. If the family had been blessed with children of only one sex, there were reasons in the Victorian age to want a child of the other. Each gender contributed to the household economy.

There were eggs to gather; fruit and vegetables to plant, harvest, and preserve; animals to tend for milk and meat; corn and wheat to grind; furniture and silver to polish; feather beds to make, and on and on. Yet those who lived in Victorian times countered their never-ending round of necessary chores with an admirable sense of purpose and strong devotion to family. The addition of a new child was truly a blessing from God.

PARENTAL RECOLLECTIONS

A child's a plaything for an hour:
Its pretty trick we try
For that or for a longer space,
Then tire and lay it by.

But I knew one that to itself
All reasons would control,
That would have mocked the sense of pain
Out of a grieved soul.

Thou struggler into loving arms,
Young climber up of knees!
When I forget thy thousand ways,
Then life and all shall cease.

Mary Lamb

*T*rain up a child in the way he should go:
and when he is old,
he will not depart from it.

Proverbs 22:6

A FATHER'S THOUGHTS

In my darling's bosom
Has dropped a living rosebud,
Fair as brilliant Hesper
Against the brimming flood.
She handles him,
She dandles him,
She fondles him and eyes him:
And if upon a tear he wakes,
With many a kiss she dries him:
She covets every move he makes,
And never enough can prize him.
Ah, the young Usurper!
I yield my golden throne:
Such angel bands attend his hands
To claim it for his own.

George Meredith

A CHILD'S INHERITANCE

Children are what the mothers are.
No fondest father's fondest care
Can fashion so the infant heart
As those creative beams that dart,
With all their hope and fear, upon
The cradle of a sleeping son.

His startled eyes with wonder see
As father near him on his knee,
Who wishes all the while to trace
The mother in his future face;
But 'tis to her alone uprise
His waking arms, to her those eyes
Open with joy and not surprise.

Walter Savage Landor

THE ORIGIN OF FAIRIES

When the first baby laughed for the first time, his laugh broke into a million pieces, and they all went skipping about. That was the beginning of fairies.

J. M. Barrie (from The Little White Bird)

AT THE MIRACLE OF A CHILD

FROM A MOTHER'S HEART
AS THE
HOME IS FASHIONED

My hopes for you are so
enormous. How can I be able to teach
you all you will need to know to go out
into the world and be the person God
has created you to be? I need wisdom
from God to know when to protect and
when to discipline. This may be even
harder than I think. I am your mother,
but God is your Heavenly Father and
he is able to do all.

*M*any make the household
but only one the home.

James Russell Lowell

DEFINITION OF HOME

*H*ome is the one place in all this world
where hearts are sure of each other. It is
the place of confidence. It is the place
where we tear off that mask of guarded
and suspicious coldness which the
world forces us to wear in self-defense,
and where we pour out the unreserved
communications of full and confiding
hearts. It is the spot where expressions
of tenderness gush out without any
sensation of awkwardness, and without
any dread of ridicule.

F. W. Robertson

*H*omes are for mothers as nests are for birds.

Arthur B. Laughlin

HOME DEFINED

Home's not merely four square walls,
Though with pictures hung and gilded;
Home is where affection calls,
Filled with shrines the heart hath builded!
Home! Go watch the faithful dove,
Sailing 'neath the heaven above us;
Home is where there's one to love!
Home is where there's one to love us!

Home's not merely roof and room,
It needs something to endear it;
Home is where the heart can bloom,
Where there's some kind lip to cheer it!
What is home with none to meet,
None to welcome, none to greet us?
Home is sweet—and only sweet—
When there's one we love to meet us!

Charles Swain

$\mathcal{B}$y the fireside still the light is shining;
The children's arms around the parents twining;
From love so sweet, oh who would roam?
Be it ever homely, home is home.

Dinah Mulock Craik

$\mathcal{H}$er office then, to rear, to teach,
Becoming as is meet and fit,
A link among the days, to knit
The generations each with each.

Alfred, Lord Tennyson

$\mathcal{B}$irdies with broken wings
Hide from each other,
But babies in trouble
Will run home to Mother.

Anonymous

$\mathcal{M}$other's kiss—sweeter this than any other thing!

William Allingham

$\mathcal{A}$ torn jacket is soon mended
but hard words bruise the heart of a child.

Henry Wadsworth Longfellow

$\mathcal{T}$he future destiny of the child
is always the work of the mother.

Napoleon Bonaparte

$\mathcal{O}$ne mother is worth a hundred schoolmasters.

Anonymous

MOTHER! HOME!

Mother! Home!—that blest refrain
Sounds through every hastening year:
All things go, but these remain.

Held in memory's jewelled chain,
Names most precious, names thrice dear:
Mother! Home!—that blest refrain.

How it sings away my pain!
How it stills my waking fear!
All things go, but these remain.

Griefs may grow and sorrows wane,
E'er that melody I hear:
Mother! Home!—that blest refrain,

Tenderness in every strain,
Thoughts to worship and revere;
All things go, but these remain.

Every night you smile again,
Every day you bring me cheer:
Mother! Home!—that blest refrain,
All things go, but these remain!

John Jarvis Holden

The Victorians thought that to be idle and useless was neither an honour nor a privilege. The habit of constant useful occupation was essential for the happiness and well-being of both men and women. It was also believed that the mind as well as the body should be constantly and usefully occupied. The importance of industry was impressed early upon the minds of children as a means of wholesome happiness in the world.

The best smell is bread,
The best savour salt,
And the best love that of children.

George Herbert

And thou shall love the Lord thy God with all tine heart, and with all thy soul, and with all thy might. . . . And thou shalt teach them diligently unto thy children, and shalt talk of them when thou sittest in thine house, and when thou walkest by the way, and when thou liest down, and when thou risest up.

Deuteronomy 6:5, 7

Once I asked my mother why she wasn't a boy like me,
So she could grow to be a man and sail upon the sea,
And be a famous commodore and have a lot of ships;
"I would rather be your mother," and her love was on her lips.

David Stearns

My world may be small, but 'tis happy
And peaceful, far from the mad whirl,
And the day's toil is lost and forgotten
In the kiss of my wee baby girl.

Louise Malloy

WHAT RULES THE WORLD

They say that man is mighty,
He governs land and sea,
He wields a mighty scepter
O'er lesser powers than he;

But mightier power and stronger
Man from his throne has hurled,
For the hand that rocks the cradle
Is the hand that rules the world.

W. R. Wallace

Money builds the house,
Mothers make the home.

George Zell

From the father comes the honor,
From the mother comfort.

Dutch Proverb

A Mother's
Weekly Work

Because of the vast amount of work required to keep a home of the Victorian era in good order, a mother had to be extremely organized. A rigid schedule was essential, regardless of whether she was the manager of others or doing the work herself.

Monday was washday. Clothes were scrubbed on a wash board or boiled to make them white, then line dried, folded, and put away.

Tuesday was ironing day. Irons were heated on top of the stove, with heavy starch used on men's collars and cuffs. Dainty baby things were kept soft.

Wednesday was mending day. Mothers were expected to mend all articles, and they had been trained by their mothers in the fine art of embroidery and clothing construction.

Thursday was for shopping.

Friday was for housecleaning.

Saturday was cooking and baking day, a time to prepare for Sunday. On Saturday night, little shoes were cleaned and polished and Sunday clothes were laid out.

Although Sunday was said to be a day of rest, Mother was up earlier than usual to ready her large family for Sunday school, church, and then for family gatherings. So for Mother, rest was elusive!

*H*ome is the grandest of all institutions.

C. H. Spurgeon

*P*oets sing of home,
Mothers sing at home.

Alfred R. Jackson

*N*o work in the world pays like mother work.

Anonymous

*W*omanliness means only motherhood;
All love begins and ends there.

Robert Browning

*W*hat is home without a mother?
　　What are all the joys we meet
When her loving smile no longer
　　Greets the coming of our feet?
The days are long, the nights are drear,
　　And time rolls slowly on;
And, oh, how few are childhood's pleasures,
　　When her loving care is gone.

Alice Hawthorne

*B*ut as for me and my house, we will serve the Lord.

Joshua 24:15

*W*here there is a mother in the house, matters speed well.

A. Bronson Alcott

CHILDHOOD'S DEAREST IMAGE

Oh, there's many a lovely picture
On memory's silent wall,
There's many a cherished image
That I tenderly recall!
The sweet home of my childhood,
With its singing brooks and birds,
The friends who grew around me,
With their loving looks and words;
The flowers that decked the wildwood,
The roses fresh and sweet,
The bluebells and the daisies
That blossomed at my feet—
All, all are very precious,
And often come to me,
Like breezes from that country
That shines beyond death's sea.
But the sweetest, dearest image
That fancy can create
Is the image of my mother,
My mother at the gate.

Matilda C. Edwards

From a Mother's Heart come Loving Counsel and Wisdom

God has shown me that motherhood is a stewardship. For a time he has lent you to me to nurture, to love, and to teach God's way.

How I pray that you will know him, that your life will be a good one, and that you will be a bearer of his grace to others. I am praying for your future even though you are barely old enough to walk.

A Mother is the truest friend we
have; when trials, heavy and sudden,
fall upon us; when adversity takes the
place of prosperity; when friends who
rejoice with us in our sunshine, desert
us when troubles thicken around us,
still will she cling to us, and endeavor
by her kind precepts and counsels to
dissipate the clouds of darkness, and
cause peace to return to our hearts.

Washington Irving

*T*he mother's heart is the child's schoolroom.

Henry Ward Beecher

*Y*outh fades, love droops, the leaves of friendship fall:
A mother's secret hope outlives them all.

Oliver Wendell Holmes

I think it must somewhere be written,
that the virtues of mothers
shall occasionally be visited on their children as well
as the sins of fathers.

Charles Dickens

*H*ear thou, my son, and be wise,
and guide thine heart in the way.

Proverbs 23:19

*T*each your child to hold his tongue,
he'll learn fast enough to speak.

Benjamin Franklin

*T*he mother, in her office, holds the key
Of the soul; and she it is who stamps the coin
Of character, and makes the being who would be a savage,
But for her gentle cares, a Christian man.

Anonymous

No language can express the power, and beauty, and heroism, and majesty of a mother's love. It shrinks not where man cowers; and grows stronger where man faints, and over the wastes of worldly fortunes sends the radiance of its quenchless fidelity like a star in heaven.

Chapin

The bearing and the training of a child is woman's wisdom.

Alfred, Lord Tennyson

A mother only knows a mother's fondness.

Lady Mary Wortley Montagu

Mother condensed into brief adages much of her wisdom which she conveniently dropped upon her children's hearts and ears throughout the day. The simplicity of her words spoke volumes and kept little souls in line, preparing them for this world and the next.

Here is a list of sayings that mothers frequently used in Victorian times:

> A place for everything and everything in
>   its place.
> Pride goeth before a fall.
> Waste not, want not.
> Idle hands are the devil's workshop.
> You are known by the company you keep.
> Bad company spoils good morals.
> Birds of a feather flock together.
> A stitch in time saves nine.
> Cleanliness is next to godliness.
> Pretty is as pretty does.
> God helps those who help themselves.
> Little pitchers have big ears.
> Children should be seen and not heard.
> The love of money is the root of all evil.
> A soft answer turneth away wrath.
> Don't put off until tomorrow what you
>   can do today.
> You can catch more flies with honey than
>   you can with vinegar.
> You get what you give in this world.

With advice like this, it was the rare child who took the wrong road.

A MOTHER UNDERSTANDS

When mother sits beside my bed
At night, and strokes and smooths my head,
And kisses me, I think, some way,
How naughty I have been all day;
Of how I waded in the brook,
And of the cookies that I took
And how I smashed a window light
A-rassling—me and Bobby White—
And tore my pants, and told a lie;
It almost makes me want to cry
When mother pats and kisses me;
I'm just as sorry as can be,
But I don't tell her so—no sir.
She knows it all; you can't fool her.

Anonymous

A father may turn his back on his child;
brothers and sisters may become inveterate
enemies, husbands may desert their wives,
and wives their husbands. But a mother's
love endures through all; in good repute, in
bad repute, in the face of the world's
condemnation, a mother still loves on, and
still hopes that her child may turn from his
evil ways and repent.

Washington Irving

A mother would rather die than see her child ruined and disgraced; and could mother-love save from the ways of sin, there would be but few travelers on the road that leads down to death.

Anonymous

*C*orrect thy son, and he shall give thee rest; yea, he shall give delight unto thy soul.

Proverbs 29:17

*P*rovoke not your children to anger, lest they be discouraged.

Colossians 3:21

THE GOODEST MOTHER

Evening was falling, cold and dark,
And people hurried along the way
As if they were longing, soon to mark
Their own home candle's cheering lay.

Before me toiled in the whirling wind
A woman with bundles great and small,
And after her tugged, a step behind,
The Bundle she loved the best of all.

A dear little roly-poly boy
With rosy cheeks, and a jacket blue,
Laughing and chattering full of joy,
And here's what he said — I tell you true:

"You're the goodest mother that ever was."
A voice as clear as a forest bird's;
And I'm sure the glad young heart had cause
To utter the sweet of the lovely words.

Perhaps the woman had worked all day
Washing or scrubbing; perhaps she sewed;
I knew, by her weary footfall's way,
That life for her was an uphill road.

But here was a comfort. Children dear,
Think what a comfort you might give
To the very best friend you can have here,
The lady fair in whose house you live,

If once in a while you stop and say —
In task or play for a moment pause —
And tell her in sweet and winning way,
"You're the goodest mother that ever was."

Anonymous

FROM A MOTHER'S HEART

And thou shalt love the Lord thy God
with all thine heart, and with all thy soul,
and with all thy might. And these words,
which I command thee this day, shall be
in thine heart: And thou shalt teach them
diligently unto thy children, and shalt talk
of them when thou sittest in thine house,
and when thou walkest by the way, and
when thou liest down, and then thou
risest up.

Deuteronomy 6:5-7

GIFT SUGGESTIONS FOR MOTHER

a bouquet of her favorite flowers
lace handkerchiefs
decorative hair combs
sachets
a piece of Mother's china or silver
a parasol
a cameo pin
framed photograph
crocheted doilies
confectionaries or chocolates
a locket
a poem written just for Mother

$\mathcal{T}$o a man there is no better support nor comfort than his mother, whose love is more nearly divine than any other human love which he can ever experience, because it is the most unselfish of all loves, and the love which is sure to remain his from the cradle to the grave.

Francis Evans

FAITHFULNESS

$\mathcal{F}$or unwearying patience and unchanging tenderness, the love of a true mother stands next to the love of our Father in heaven.

Anonymous

NO OTHER WORD

$\mathcal{T}$here's no other word that's spoken 'neath the starry sky above,
Can so touch our hearts as "Mother" or inspire so pure a love.
It awakened with our being, and in sweet maternal ways,
It was hallowed as 'twas nurtured in our happy childhood days.
In our eyes and thoughts no other has so kind and saintly face,
And of all we fondly cherish, none can ever fill her place.

E. B. Grimes

WALKING ALONE

*I*t was prettily said by a young mother, "When my little son began to walk alone, I felt that he was breaking away from me." It is a painful blow this first attempted detachment, which the child will later on renew at each fresh outburst of his youth. . . ."He used to steady himself against the furniture, to clutch hold of my dress, then one day he pulls himself together, tries his unsteady little steps, balances himself, and off he goes! Oh, how I cried!"

Mme. Alphonse Daudet

*O*ur lives are albums, written through
With good or ill, with false or true;
And as the blessed angels turn
The pages of our years.
God, grant they read the good with smiles,
And blot the bad with tears.

John Milton

He who takes the child by the hand, takes
the mother by the heart.

Danish Proverb

Let France have good mothers
and she will have good sons.

Napoleon Bonaparte

QUEEN OF BABYLAND

Who is queen of Babyland?
Mother kind and sweet,
And her love, born above,
Guides the little feet.

George Cooper

The world has no such flower in any land,
And no such pearl in any gulf the sea,
As any babe on any mother's knee.

Algernon Charles Swinburne

FROM A MOTHER'S HEART COME PRAYERS AND LULLABIES

This is my favorite time of day. As we kneel beside the bed together with your little head bowed, I teach you the first simple prayers of childhood. It is a peaceful time, a sweet time, and a time to cherish. It is the first time you have been still all day! Five more "God blesses," one more glass of water, and our day is done.

THE MOTHER'S PRAYER

Dear Lord, dear Lord. . . .
Thou, who didst not erst deny
The mother-joy to Mary mild
Blessed in the blessed Child —
Hearkening in meek babyhood
Her cradle hymn, albeit used
To all that music interfused
In breasts of angels high and good.
Oh, take not, Lord, my babe away —
Oh, take not to thy songful heaven,
The pretty babe thou hast given;
Or ere that I have seen him play
Around his father's knee, and known
That he knew how my love hath gone
From all the world to him.

Elizabeth Barrett Browning

At first babes feed on the mother's bosom,
but always on her heart.

Henry Ward Beecher

*I*n the Victorian home, there was, out of
necessity, an order and a time for everything.
   So it also followed that there was a routine to
establish the sleeping habits of the small children of
the household.

   To give the children a feeling of security and
discipline, a fixed time was set for naps and bedtime.

   The mood was set by drawing the curtains and
perhaps singing a lullaby. Being crooned to sleep
shortened the way to the Land of Nod. As Mr.
Sandman slowly closed the eyes, the mother and
child rocked gently together during one of the
sweetest moments of the day.

   All cultures have a tradition of mothers singing
lullabies and baby songs to their children. The very
term *lullaby* has a soothing sound and conveys what
it means perhaps better than any other word in our
language.

   Poetic refrains were passed from generation to
generation with some spontaneously composed as a
mother rocked her little one to sleep. The calming
rhythm of the words combined with the rocking
motion, and the warmth of the mother's breast
carried the child into peaceful slumber with sweet
dreams and visions of angels keeping watch.

   As the child grew, this time of day became a time
for prayer, reading, and reflection.

   Parents frequently joined together at the bedside
to hear their child's prayers. Kneeling beside the bed,
the child often sang these first prayers to the tune of
a favorite hymn. These early spiritual lessons in a
child's life taught many important things: bowing the
knee to God in respect and adoration, thanksgiving
for every good and perfect gift, and learning to pray
for the needs of others.

HOLY INNOCENTS

Sleep, little baby, sleep,
  The holy angels love thee,
And guard thy bed and keep
  A blessed watch above thee.
No spirit can come near
  Nor evil beast to harm thee;
Sleep, sweet, devoid of fear
  Where nothing need alarm thee.

The love which doth not sleep,
  The eternal arms surround thee:
The shepherd of true sheep
  In perfect love hath found thee.
Sleep through the holy night,
  Christ-kept from snare and sorrow,
Until thou wake to light
  And love and warmth tomorrow.

Christina Rossetti

The mother yields her babe to sleep
Upon her tender breast,
And sings a lullaby, to keep
Its little heart at rest.

O sweet unto my heart is the song my
  mother sings
As eventide is brooding on its dark and
  noiseless wings!
Every note is charged with memory—every
  memory bright with rays
Of the golden hour of promise in the lap of
  childhood's days.
The orchard blooms anew, and each blossom
  scents the way,
And I feel again the breath of eve among
  the new-mown hay;
While through the halls of memory in happy
  notes there rings
All the life-joy of the past in the song my
  mother sings.

Thomas O'Hagan

LULLABY

Softly sleep, my darling,
   on your little bed;
Kindly guardian angels,
   Hover round thy head.
Be your infant visions
   Sweet and bright as they
Wake with childish laughter
   At the break of day.

LULLABY

Lullaby, oh lullaby!
Flowers are closed and lambs are sleeping;
   Lullaby, oh lullaby!
Stars are up, the moon is peeping;
   Lullaby, oh lullaby!
While the birds are silence keeping,
   Lullaby, oh lullaby!
Sleep, my baby, fall a-sleeping,
   Lullaby, oh lullaby!

Christina Rossetti

LULLABY

Dream, baby, dream! the stars are glowing;
  Hear'st thou the stream so softly flowing?
  All gently glide the hours,
  Above no tempest lowers,
  Below are fragrant flowers
In silence growing.
Dream, baby, dream!

Sleep, baby, sleep, till dawn tomorrow;
Why should'st thou weep who know'st not sorrow?
  Too soon come pains and fears,
  Too soon a chase for tears,
  So from thy future years
No sadness borrow.
Sleep, baby, sleep!

Barry Cornwall

CRADLE SONG

Sleep, baby, sleep,
Thy father is tending sheep.
Thy mamma is shaking the dreamland tree
And down drops a little dream on thee.
Sleep, baby, sleep.

Sleep, baby, sleep,
I will buy for thce a sheep
With a golden bell, so fine to see.
And it shall run and play with thee.
Sleep, baby, sleep.

Sleep, baby, sleep,
The large stars are the sheep.
And the little stars are the lambs, I guess,
And the fair moon is the shepherdess.
Sleep, baby, sleep

Sleep, baby, sleep,
Dear Jesus loves the sheep.
And thou his little lamb shalt be
and in his breast he'll carry thee.
Sleep, baby, sleep

German Folksong

A CRADLE HYMN

*H*ush! my dear, lie still and slumber,
Holy angels guard thy bed!
Heavenly blessings without number
Gently falling on thy head.

Soft and easy is thy cradle:
Coarse and hard thy Saviour lay,
When His birthplace was a stable
And His softest bed was hay.

See the lovely babe a-dressing;
Lovely infant, how He smiled!
When He wept, the mother's blessing
Soothed and hush'd the holy Child.

Lo, He slumbers in His manger,
Where the horned oxen fed;
Peace, my darling; here's no danger,
Here's no ox a-near thy bed.

Isaac Watts

THE CHILD AT PRAYER

A baby to a Baby prays,
Oh, Infant Jesus, meek and mild,
From 'mid the glory and the rays,
Look on a little child.

As one child to another may,
He talks without a thought of fear;
Commending to a child today
All that a child holds dear:

His father, mother, brother, nurse,
His cat, his dog, his bird, his toys:
Things that make up the universe
Of darling girls and boys.

All sheep and horses, lambs, and cows,
He counts them o'er, a motley crew;
And children in the neighbor's house
And all the people too.

His friends—why, all the world's his friend;
This four-years' darling, golden curled,
'Tis long before it has an end,
The bed-roll of his world.

A child lifts up his little hands
Unto a Child; and it may be
The Host of Heaven at gazing stands
That tender sight to see.

Katharine Tynan Hinkson

ALL THROUGH THE NIGHT

Sleep my child and peace attend thee
All through the night.
Guardian angels God will send thee
All Through the night.
Soft the drowsy hours are creeping,
Hill and vale in slumber sleeping,
I my loving vigil keeping,
All through the night.

While the moon her watch is keeping
All through the night.
While the weary world is sleeping,
All through the night.
O'er thy spirit gently stealing,
Visions of delight revealing,
Breathes a pure and holy feeling
All through the night.

HYMN FOR A LITTLE CHILD

God make my life a little light
Within the world to glow;
A little flame that burneth bright
Wherever I may go.

God make my life a little flower
That giveth joy to all;
Content to bloom in native bower,
Although its place be small.

God make my life a little song
That comforteth the sad;
That helpeth others to be strong,
And makes the singer glad.

God make my life a little staff
Whereon the weak may rest,
That so what health or strength I have,
May serve my neighbor best.

God make my life a little hymn,
Of tenderness and praise,
Of faith that never waxeth dim,
In all his wondrous ways.

Anonymous

$\mathcal{T}$he melodies of many lands erewhile
    have charmed mine ear,
Yet there's but one among them all which
    still my heart holds dear;
I heard it first from lips I loved, my tears
    it then beguiled;
It was the song my mother sang when I was
    but a child.

C. W. Glover

THE SOOTHING SOUND
OF MOTHER'S VOICE

The earliest and most consistent sounds an infant heard were uttered by the child's mother. And the baby's first introduction to music was most often that of a mother's singing as she rocked and held her small child.

Music in the Victorian home included many hymns and songs with Christian content. The division we have today between adult hymns and children's hymns and songs did not exist, and from a child's earliest days, a mother sang to her baby the hymns she loved.

"He Leadeth Me" and "Sweet Hour of Prayer," both by William Batchelder Bradbury, indicate sincere dependence on the Lord and a close relationship with Him. It was also during this period that Phillips Brooks, the great preacher from Boston, composed "O Little Town of Bethlehem," and William Howard Doane wrote "Tell Me the Old, Old Story." One can easily imagine a young mother rocking her child and singing these hymns to the little one.

I remember my mother's prayers
and they have always followed me.
They have clung to me all my life.

Abraham Lincoln

A PRAYER FOR MOTHERS

*L*ord, give the mothers of the world
    More love to do their part;
That love which reaches not alone
The children made by birth their own,
    But every childish heart.
Wake in their souls true motherhood,
Which aims at universal good.

Ella Wheeler Wilcox

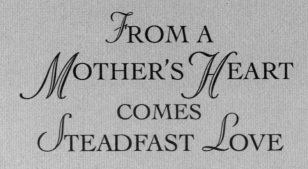

FROM A
MOTHER'S HEART
COMES
STEADFAST LOVE

When you stray, I may not approve; I may lecture you or even discipline you—but I will always love you.

When you test your wings, I must remember that some lessons in life must be learned the hard way. How painful it is for me to watch. There is something in a mother that wants to kiss away every hurt and make everything right.

Yet I know I cannot be all things to you. As the old proverb says, "It takes an entire village to raise a child."

Forbearing one another
in love.
Eph. 4. 2.

Be kind one to another.
Eph. 4. 32.

$\mathcal{G}$od could not be everywhere;
therefore He made mothers.

Hebrew Proverb

$\mathcal{A}$s one whom his mother comforteth, so will I comfort you.

Isaiah 66:13

$\mathcal{M}$other is the name for God
in the lips and heart of little children.

William Makepeace Thackeray

$\mathcal{H}$eaven is kind, as a noble mother.

Thomas Carlyle

During the Victorian era, the strong father figure was the king of his castle and ruled supreme in the home. Even though father was the spiritual head of the family, mother's role and influence in the lives of her children were of utmost importance. It was she more than any other who formed the character of her children. She created the moral atmosphere in which they lived and by which their hearts and minds were nourished. She cherished the infant, instructed the child, was the guide and counselor of youth and the confidante and companion of adulthood.

She was the living example to her children of self-denial, perseverance, dedication, and devotion. Her influence, affecting the children, in turn affected all of society. The influence of both mother and father was strong, but the mother's influence was mainly on the heart.

There is no love like a mother's —
'Tis the sun that shineth forth;
There is no truth like a mother's —
'Tis the star that points the North;
There is no hope like a mother's —
'Tis the April in the clod;
There is no trust like a mother's —
'Tis the charity of God:
The love and truth, the hope and trust
That make the mortal more than dust.

John Jarvis Holden

A partnership with God is motherhood;
What strength, what purity, what self-control,
What love, what wisdom should belong to her,
Who helps God fashion an immortal soul.

Anonymous

Soft be the hour of the sleeping,
Little one mine, dear little one mine.
Safe, gentle lamb, be thy keeping
In the arms of the shepherd divine.
Fond as thy mother's love,
Yet there is one above
Loves thee still dearer —
And when for thee she prays
Grace, peace, and happy days —
Bends down to hear her.

W. Calvert

In the heavens above, the angels
whispering to one another, can find,
amid their burning terms of love,
none so devotional as that of
"mother."

Edgar Allan Poe

The real religion of the world comes
from women much more than from
men—from mothers most of all, who
carry the key of our souls in their
bosoms.

Oliver Wendell Holmes

There is a religion in all deep love,
but the love of a mother
is a veil of a softer light
between the heart and the Heavenly Father.

Samuel Taylor Coleridge

God pardons like a mother,
Kisses the offence into everlasting forgetfulness.

Henry Ward Beecher

MY MOTHER'S KNEE

There was a place in childhood that I
    remember well,
And there a voice of sweetest tone bright
    fairy tales did tell;
And gentle words and fond embrace were
    given with joy to me
When I was in that happy place, upon my
    mother's knee.

When fairy tales were ended, "Good
    night," she softly said,
And kissed, and laid me down to sleep
    within my tiny bed;
And holy words she taught me there
    methinks I yet can see
Her angel eyes, as close I knelt beside my
    mother's knee.

In the sickness of my childhood, the perils
    of my prime,
The sorrows of my riper years, the cares
    of every time;
When doubt and danger weighed me
    down, the pleading all for me,
It was a fervent prayer to heaven that
    bent my mother's knee.

Samuel Lover

A mother's love — the dearest love
that God ever gave to mortal creatures.

Charles Dickens

O MAGICAL WORD

O magical word may it never die
    From the lips that love to speak it,
Nor melt away from the trusting hearts
    That even would break to keep it.
Was there ever a name that lived like thine?
    Will there ever be another?
The angels have reared in heaven a shrine
    To the holy name of mother.

Anonymous

*L*ong, long before the babe could speak,
And to her bosom press,
The brightest angels standing near
Would turn away to hide a tear—
For they were motherless.

John Banister Tabb

*E*ven He that died for us upon the cross,
in the last hour, in the unutterable agony
of death, was mindful of His mother, as if
to teach us that this holy love should be
our last worldly thought—the last point of
earth from which the soul should take its
flight for Heaven.

Henry Wadsworth Longfellow

A Mother's love, the best love;
God's love, the highest love.

German Proverb

*H*e who helps a child helps humanity with a distinctness,
with an immediateness,
which no other help
given to human creatures
in any other stage of their human life
can possibly give again.

Phillips Brooks

MOTHER'S LOVE

What is there down so deep,
 But mother's love will find it?
Cover it over and hide it well,
Neither with lips, nor by glances tell;
Have you a trouble? Wherever it dwell,
 Mother's love finds it out.

What is there up so high,
 But mother's love can share it?
All that is noble, and good and true,
That which enriches and blesses you,
What you accomplish, and purpose to do,
 Mother's love shares it all.

Is anything too hard
 For mother to do for you?
No, obstacles vanish, and cares grow light,
Dangers diminish, and clouds become bright,
Burdens grow small, and roll out of sight
 For mother when doing for you.

Anonymous

A mother is a mother still,
The holiest thing alive.

Samuel Taylor Coleridge

*N*ever comes mortal utterance so near to
eternity as when a child utters words of
loving praise to a mother! Every syllable
drops into the jewel box of her memory,
to be treasured for ever and ever.

George B. Lyon

THE MOTHER

*G*od thought to give the sweetest thing
In His almighty power
To earth; and deeply pondering
What it should be, one hour
In fondest joy and love of heart
Outweighing every other,
He moved the gates of Heaven apart
And gave to earth—a mother!

G. Newell Lovejoy

MOTHER'S LOVE

By her my lisping tongue in prayer
Was taught to bless the God of light,
Her kindness soothed my childish care,
And watched my slumbers during night.
Poor is the immortal sculptor's art,
The painter's pencil, poet's song,
Compared to her who moulds the heart
With plastic hand while pure and young.
A sister's love is warm and kind,
A brother's strong as hand of time;
And sweet the love of kindred mind,
But, Mother, these are not like thine.

Dear Mother, from thy home above,
Still come and bless me with thy love.

John S. Reid

There are soft words murmured by dear, dear lips,
Far richer than any other:
But the sweetest word that the ear hath heard
Is the blessed name of "Mother."

O magical word may it never die
From the lips that love to speak it,
Nor melt away from the trusting hearts
That even would break to keep it.

Was there ever a name that lived like this?
Will there ever be such another?
The angels have reared in heaven a shrine
To the holy name of "Mother."

Anonymous

Ah, then how sweetly closed those crowded days!
The minutes parting one by one like rays
That fade upon a summer's eve.
But, oh, what charm, or magic numbers
Can give me back the gentle slumbers
Those weary, happy days did leave?
When by my bed I saw my mother kneel,
And with her blessing took her nightly kiss;
Whatever Time destroys, he cannot this —
E'en now that nameless kiss I feel.

Washington Allston

From a Mother's Heart as Mother is Remembered

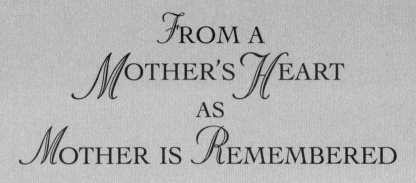

When I was a child, my mother was the center of my world. I looked to her for every need. As I grew into my teenage years, I became too smart for my mother. When I reached my twenties, I realized how smart my mother had become in the last ten years. When I became a mother myself, I knew the scope of her love and the depth of her wisdom.

The goal of my life is to be the kind of mother that my mother was to me.

Memories of mothers are sweet,
but never as sweet as mothers themselves.
Some of us forget this.

M. D. Hillmer

A man never knows all that his mother has been to him
till it's too late to let her know that he sees it.

William Dean Howells

Stories first heard at a mother's knee
are never wholly forgotten—
a little spring that never quite dries up
in our journey through scorching years.

Ruffini

A mother's heart, like primroses,
opens most beautifully
in the evening of life.

Anonymous

One Among Hundreds

Hundreds of stars in the pretty sky,
Hundreds of shells on the shore together,
Hundreds of birds that go singing by,
Hundred of birds in the sunny weather,

Hundreds of dewdrops to greet the dawn,
Hundreds of bees in the purple clover,
Hundreds of butterflies on the lawn,
But only one mother the wide world over.

Ira M. Webster

And God shall wipe away all tears from
their eyes; and there shall be no more
death, neither sorrow, nor crying, neither
shall there be any more pain: for the
former things are passed away.

Revelation 21:4

When I am sad it comes to me,
  A tender quiet old strain;
I hear her voice soft, low, and sweet,
  Take up the song again,
I lean and listen to the sound —
  Were ever notes like these?
Like brooding thrush, at sunset hour,
  When day is at its close.

Old, sad and worn, a man of care,
  Life grows confused to me;
The things that were I have forgot,
  Nor care for things to be.
Yet, through the halls of memory,
  Comes back that old, old strain,
I am a boy — my mother sings
  Her old-time song again.

Emma M. Johnson

$\mathcal{A}$ll that I am my mother made me.

John Quincy Adams

$\mathcal{A}$ mother's love is indeed the golden link that binds youth to age; and he is still but a child, however time may have furrowed his cheek, or silvered his brow, who can yet recall the gentle chidings, of the best friend that God ever gives us.

Bovee

$\mathcal{M}$y mother was as mild as any saint, And nearly canonized by all she knew, So gracious was her tact and tenderness.

Alfred, Lord Tennyson

When we think of the Victorian life, we associate it with beauty, refinement, gentility, morality, and elegance. The darker side of this picture is the brevity of life then. The average lifespan in America was twenty-eight years. The highest incidence of death was in infants, largely because of rudimentary medical knowledge. It was a rare family that had not lost at least one child to death, so children were celebrated. Christenings, their birthdays, and all holidays were occasions of great familial joy, as there was an overabundance of death surrounding them.

Comparing one man with another,
You'll find the maxim true,
That the man who is good to his mother
Will always be good to you!

Fred Emerson Brooks

MY MOTHER

I walk upon the rocky shore,
Her strength is in the ocean's roar.
I glance into the shaded pool,
Her mind is there so calm and cool.
I hear sweet rippling of the sea,
Naught but her laughter 'tis to me.
I gaze into the starry skies,
And there I see her wondrous eyes.
I look into my inmost mind,
And here her inspiration find.
In all I am and hear and see,
My precious mother is with me.

Josephine Rice Creelman

ROCK ME TO SLEEP

Backward, turn backward, O Time, in your flight,
Make me a child again, just for tonight!
Mother, come back from the echoless shore,
Take me again to your heart, as of yore;
Kiss from my forehead the furrows of care,
Smooth the few silver threads out of my hair,
Over my slumbers your loving watch keep;
Rock me to sleep, Mother, rock me to sleep.

Come, let your brown hair, just lighted with gold,
Fall on your shoulders again as of old;
Let it drop over my forehead tonight,
Shading my faint eyes away from the light;
For with its sunny-edged shadows once more
Haply will throng the sweet visions of yore;
Lovingly, softly, its bright billows sweep;
Rock me to sleep, Mother, rock me to sleep.

Mother, dear Mother, the years have been long
Since I last listened to your lullaby song:
Sing, then, and unto my soul it shall seem
Womanhood's years have been only a dream.
Clasped to your heart in a loving embrace,
With your light lashes just sweeping my face,
Never hereafter to wake or to weep;
Rock me to sleep, Mother, rock me to sleep!

Elizabeth Akers Allen

Where crystal streams through endless years
Flow over golden sands,
And where the old grow young again,
I'll clasp my mother's hands.

Ellen M. H. Gates

To every thing there is a season,
and a time to every purpose under the heaven:
a time to be born, and a time to die.

Ecclesiastes 3:1-2

There was no family therapy or professional counseling in those days. To deal with death, the Victorians developed their own means of grieving. True to the Victorian form they developed a ritual of mourning. This involved etiquette, rules, and observances.

There was a deep mourning period of one to two years during which mourning attire was usually simple in design. Black in the beginning, it changed to gray as the period of mourning came to a close.

Brief letters of condolence were sent to those in affliction, offering affectionate sympathy and religious comfort. It was proper for the bereaved to use black-bordered stationery, the edge being broad at the onset of mourning and gradually becoming narrower.

Viewing of the deceased as well as the funeral service often took place in the home. Intimate friends and relatives would observe visitations, not only at the time of death but also the month following.

The deceased was immortalized with memorial cards frequently personalized with a small cameo photograph. It was not uncommon for a professional photographer to make elaborate pictures of the deceased in repose within the casket and surrounded by flowers.

Locks of hair were sometimes placed in lockets or braided into jewelry or hair wreaths.

Books were written as memorials to beloved mothers and poems about empty cradles and mothers' tears were commonplace. While this seems a bit morbid to those living in our day these observances served as aids for emotional survival.

The Victorians believed that to live in hearts left behind is not to die.

Dear beacon of my childhood's day,
   The lodestar of my youth,
A mingled glow of tenderest love
   And firm, unswerving truth,
I've wandered far o'er east and west,
   'Neath many stranger skies,
But ne'er I've seen a fairer light
   Than that in mother's eyes.

L. M. Montgomery

Blessed is the memory of an old-fashioned mother. It floats to us now, like the beautiful perfume of some woodland blossoms. The music of other voices may be lost, but the entrancing melody of hers will echo in our souls forever. Other faces will fade away and be forgotten, but hers will shine on until the light from Heaven's portals will glorify our own.

Anonymous

If e'er from human bliss or woe
I feel the sympathetic glow;
If e'er my heart hath learned to know
The generous wish or prayer,
Who sowed the germ with tender hand?
Who marked its infant leaves expand?
My mother's fostering care.
And if one flower of charms refined
May grace the garden of my mind,
'Twas she who nursed it there.
She loved to cherish and adorn
Each blossom of the soil,
To banish every weed and thorn,
That oft opposed her toil.

Felicia Dorothea Hemans

What is learned in the cradle lasts till the grave.

French Proverb

*A*ll women become like their mothers.
That is their tragedy.
No man does. That is his.

Oscar Wilde

*T*he mother makes us most.

Alfred, Lord Tennyson

*B*lessed be the God and Father of our
Lord Jesus Christ, which according to his
abundant mercy hath begotten us again
unto a lively hope by the resurrection of
Jesus Christ from the dead.

1 Peter 1:3

$\mathcal{G}$od sends us children for another purpose than merely to keep up the race: to enlarge our hearts; to make us unselfish, and full of kindly sympathies and affections; to give our souls higher aims, and to call out all our faculties to extend enterprise and exertion; they bring round our firesides bright faces, and happy smiles, and loving, tender hearts.

Mary Howitt

$\mathcal{H}$er children arise up, and call her blessed; her husband also, and he praiseth her.

Many daughters have done virtuously, but thou excellest them all.

Favour is deceitful, and beauty is vain: but a woman that feareth the Lord, she shall be praised.

Give her of the fruit of her hands; and let her own works praise her in the gates.

Proverbs 31:28-31

*H*e who passes a day of his manhood
without remembering his mother's eyes, as
they looked to him in childhood, is losing
the best part of remembrance.

Anonymous

*H*ow many there are who look back
regretfully to the days of their childhood,
and wish they were children again. That
seems to them the happiest portion of
human life—so free from cares, so buoyant
in spirits, so easily satisfied with its little
sports and pastimes. As they think of those
happy days, they almost wish they could
have remained children. Such persons
surely indulge but lowly aspirations, and but
petty views of what constitutes happiness
for rational beings. Childhood is indeed
beautiful in its season; but chiefly so in its
relations to the after years.

Anonymous

THE ORIGIN OF
MOTHER'S DAY

Like many events, the designation of a special day to honour mothers seemed to spring from several areas in Victorian times.

In 1872, Julia Ward Howe made the first known suggestion for a Mother's Day in the United States, and for several years she held an annual Mother's Day meeting in Boston. Celebrations were also begun in Kentucky and Indiana.

But it was not until 1907 that Anna Jarvis of Grafton, West Virginia, began a campaign for the observance of Mother's Day on a national level. She chose the second Sunday in May and began the custom of wearing a flower in honor of one's mother. President Woodrow Wilson gave Mother's Day recognition as an annual national holiday in 1915.

The observance continues in families and churches all across the country. If a person wears a red flower, usually a rose or carnation, it means that the mother is living. If a white flower is worn, then she is deceased.

Thus, Mother is honored in a visible and meaningful way.

FROM A LETTER WRITTEN TO MISS ANNA JARVIS, FOUNDER OF MOTHERS' DAY

*T*he heaven that lies about us in our infancy is motherhood, and no matter how exalted or how depraved we may become, we are always attended by the grace of a mother's love.

On this day let each of us honor the hallowed memory of his mother, wearing in token thereof the floral symbol of purity. Of other blessings we may have had great stores, but of that most precious influence there was but one.

James Whitcomb Riley
January 29, 1912

Memories of my Mother

....
....
....
....
....
....
....
....
....
....
....
....
....
....
....
....
....
....
....

Memories

....
....
....
....
....
....
....
....
....
....
....
....
....
....
....
....
....
....
....
....
....
....
....

Memories

....
....
....
....
....
....
....
....
....
....
....
....
....
....
....
....
....
....
....
....
....
....
....

Memories

....
....
....
....
....
....
....
....
....
....
....
....
....
....
....
....
....
....
....
....
....
....
....
....

Memories

....
....
....
....
....
....
....
....
....
....
....
....
....
....
....
....
....
....
....
....
....
....
....

....
....
....
....
....
....
....
....
....
....
....
....
....
....
....
....
....
....
....
....
....

Memories

....
....
....
....
....
....
....
....
....
....
....
....
....
....
....
....
....
....
....
....
....
....
....
....

Annette Crivella Williams was born in Punxsutawney, Pennsylvania, and grew up in Alexandria, Virginia. She attended Emory and Henry College in Emory, Virginia. During her years as a flight attendant with American Airlines, she began collecting Victorian laces, antique linens, and ephemera. An avid art lover, she has studied and taught art and exhibited her extensive collection in galleries throughout Middle Tennessee.

Annette resides in Nashville, Tennessee, with her husband, Jake.

Haden Harris Pickel, a native of Montgomery, Alabama, graduated from Auburn University with a degree in the visual arts. Haden has taught art, designed needlepoint, and exhibited her paintings in galleries in Middle Tennessee.

She and her husband, Jimmy, have two grown sons and live in Nashville, Tennessee, where she is a Bible study teacher and an avid gardener.

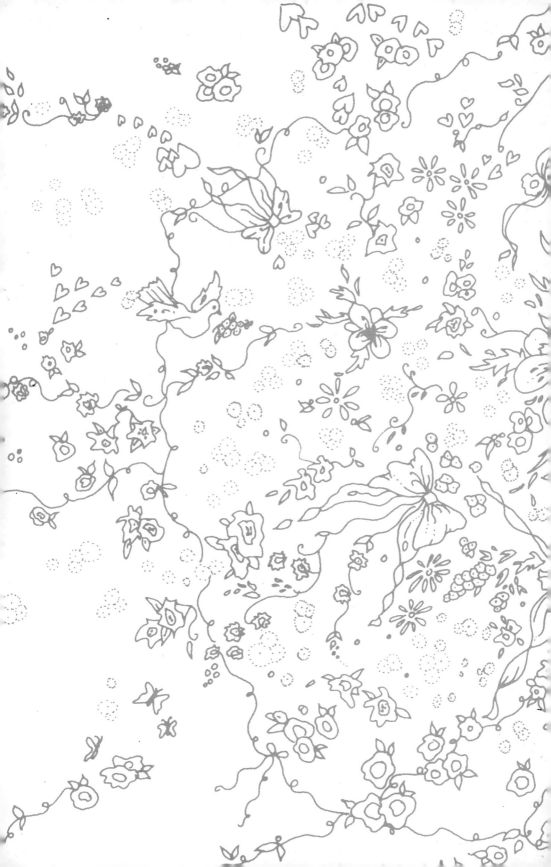